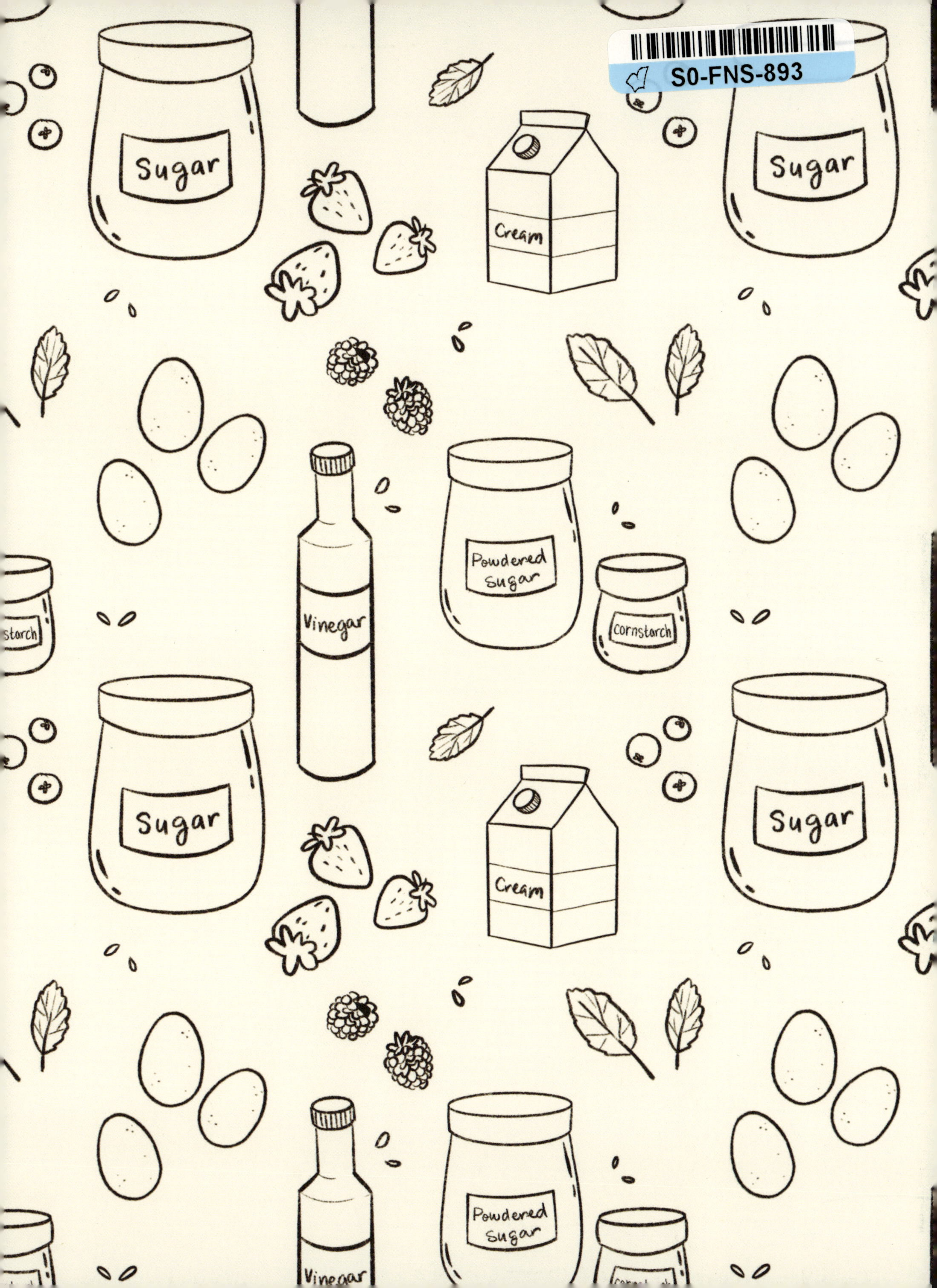
Sugar
Cream
Powdered sugar
Vinegar
cornstarch

Sugar
Sugar
Cream
Powdered sugar
cornstarch
Vinegar
Vinegar
Sugar
Sugar
Cream
Powdered sugar

Meet
Lottie

Lottie is a kind-hearted and polite little girl.
She is caring and considerate towards all animals and people but especially
has a soft spot for babies and the elderly. She loves horses, drawing, playing
with her brothers, and most of all, baking in the kitchen with Mommy.

For Ryan, Charlotte, and Rowan, who make family traditions wondrously memorable.

Lottie and the Christmas Wreath
Text copyright © 2019, 2021 Rose Bakewell
Illustrations copyright ©2022 Joannie Studio

All rights reserved. No part of this book may be used or reproduced in any manner whatsoever without written permission except in the case of brief quotations embodied in critical articles and reviews.

Hardcover: 978-1-7366557-3-3

Author and Creative director: Rose Bakewell
Illustrator: Joannie Laroche
Copy editor: Mark Farrell

Publisher: Country Cottage Books

Country Cottage Books

Daddy · Mommy · Brodie · Lottie · Kingsley

Lottie
and the Christmas Wreath

By

Rose Bakewell

Illustrated by
Joannie Laroche

It was a busy Christmas Eve in the Montgomery household. Lottie and Brodie were helping Mommy prep Christmas lunch for the next day while Daddy was playing peek-a-boo with Kingsley.

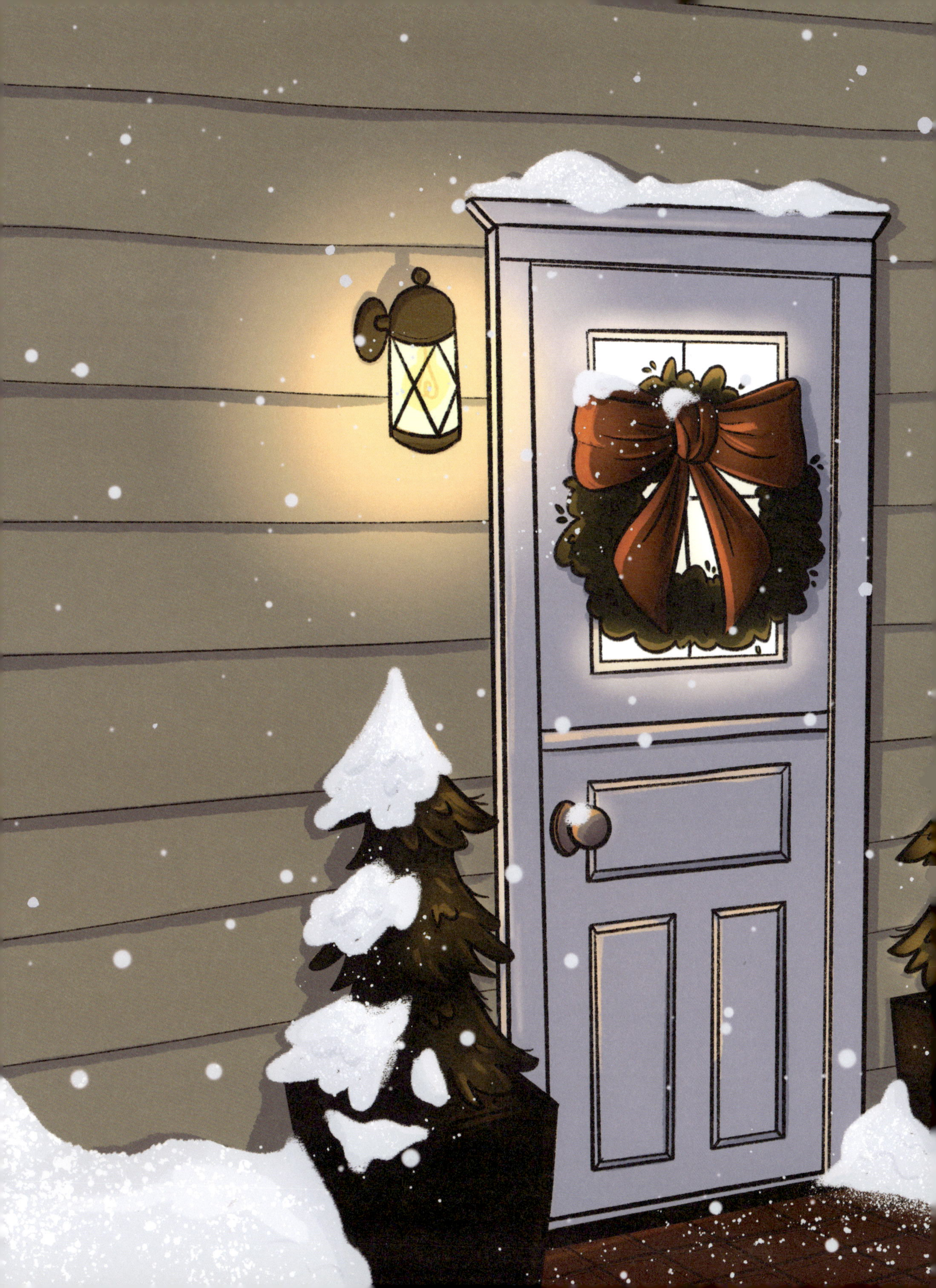

"I've rinsed all the fruits and vegetables," Brodie said. "Is there anything else you'd like me to do?"

"I think we've covered everything," Mommy replied. "All we need to do is make the pavlova, and everything else can be made tomorrow morning."

"I'm sure Lottie would do a much better job at making that than I would," he said, giving Mommy a hint.

Mommy knew Brodie's mind was on the new video game Grandpa Leo had given him as an early Christmas gift.

"Alright," she said, "You can run along and play."

"Thank you!" Brodie exclaimed and ran to the family room to grab his remote controls.

"Lottie, would you like to help me make the pavlova?" asked Mommy.

Pavlova was one of Lottie's favorite desserts. She loved the crisp meringue shell and gooey marshmallow center. She had helped Mommy make pavlova enough times to know what to do.

"I have a better idea!" Lottie said. "May I make it all by myself?"

Mommy thought it was wonderful that Lottie wanted to challenge herself, so she brought the mixer to the counter and wrote the recipe and method on a sheet of paper for Lottie to follow.

It read:

- Separate the **egg** yolks and whites (store the yolks in the refrigerator)

Whisk the **egg whites** on high speed until it forms soft peaks.

- With the mixer on medium speed, add the **sugar**, one tablespoon at a time, waiting 30 seconds in between adding each spoonful.

- Mix the **vinegar** and **cornstarch** in a small bowl and stir it into the glossy meringue mix.

Lottie followed the instructions and then scooped heaping spoonfuls of the meringue onto the baking sheet covered with parchment paper. She smoothed it into a large circular ring and made a trench in the meringue with a small spatula.

"That looks perfect!" Mommy said as she walked by. "I'll pop it in the oven, and you can go play."

"I made the pavlova all by myself!" Lottie said, gleaming at Brodie, who was focused on the video game. "Cool!" he said, without taking his eyes off the TV.

"Can I play too?" she asked.

Lottie was having so much fun that she forgot to check on the pavlova and went straight to bed after the game.

The next morning, Lottie woke up bright and early but had a strange feeling there was something she was forgetting.

CHARLOTTE

"My pavlova!" she shrieked, running to the kitchen.

Lottie opened the oven door, and the once-smooth and shiny white meringue had now lost its shine and had small cracks.

It's ruined! I've ruined Christmas dessert! She thought.

In a panic, she gathered the ingredients to make another pavlova before anybody else would be up.

But the clinging and clanging of the bowls had woken up Mommy, and she came downstairs to see what the commotion was all about.

Lottie felt awful about ruining the dessert and for attempting to cover it up by making a new one.

She broke into tears and told Mommy what had happened and how very sorry she was about everything.

"Oh, sweetheart," Mommy comforted her. "You haven't ruined anything. The pavlova turned out lovely!"

"But I forgot about it in the oven," Lottie murmured, "and now it has cracks all over it."

"Well, aren't you lucky then to have a mother who always keeps an eye on the oven?" Mommy teased.

"Sometimes," she continued, "small cracks are just part of the charm of a pavlova. Once you cover it with cream and fruits, nobody will notice them."

Mommy explained how allowing the pavlova to cool in the oven is actually better to prevent the sudden temperature change from shocking the meringue and causing it to crack even more.

"As for secretly trying to make a new pavlova, it was quick thinking, but you could have just come to me. Everyone makes mistakes, and it's okay to ask for help," she said.

Lottie was embarrassed for not being honest but felt relieved that she could always ask for help without being judged.

After breakfast, Lottie decorated the pavlova. First, she used the hand mixer to whisk the **heavy cream** until it was thick and fluffy. Then, she filled the trench with whipped cream and placed some **strawberries**, **blueberries**, and **raspberries** on top.

"Mommy!" Lottie called out. "It sort of looks like a wreath!"

"It does!" Mommy agreed.

Lottie added some **red currants** and **mint leaves** and gave it a quick dusting of **powdered sugar** to make it look like freshly fallen snow. It truly looked like a Christmas wreath.

Guests arrived one after the other, and soon, the entire house was full of family members enjoying Christmas lunch together:

Granny Beth

Grandpa Will

Auntie Emily

Uncle Henry

Grandma Jane

Grandpa Leo

Uncle George

Auntie Isla

Cousin Mary

Cousin Annie

Cousin Nick

"Should we bring out the dessert?" Mommy whispered to Lottie. Lottie nodded and helped get the plates and utensils.

Everyone gasped. "Oh, Catherine, you've outdone yourself," Granny Beth said, gazing at the dessert.

"Actually," Mommy said proudly, "it was Lottie—she made it herself."

Lottie took a bite of her pavlova, and the crisp meringue melted in her mouth, and the middle was soft and marshmallowy—just as it should be.

Everyone enjoyed Lottie's creation, especially Kingsley.

"Is it yummy, Kingsley?" Lottie asked her baby brother.

"Yummy payooba!" Kingsley said, delighted.

"The sweet meringue and tart berries go perfectly together," said Grandma Jane.

"It looks like Lottie will be making the Christmas dessert from now on," Grandpa Will added.

Lottie looked around and was overjoyed at what a success her Christmas Wreath turned out to be. "I sure will," Lottie responded as she took another bite.

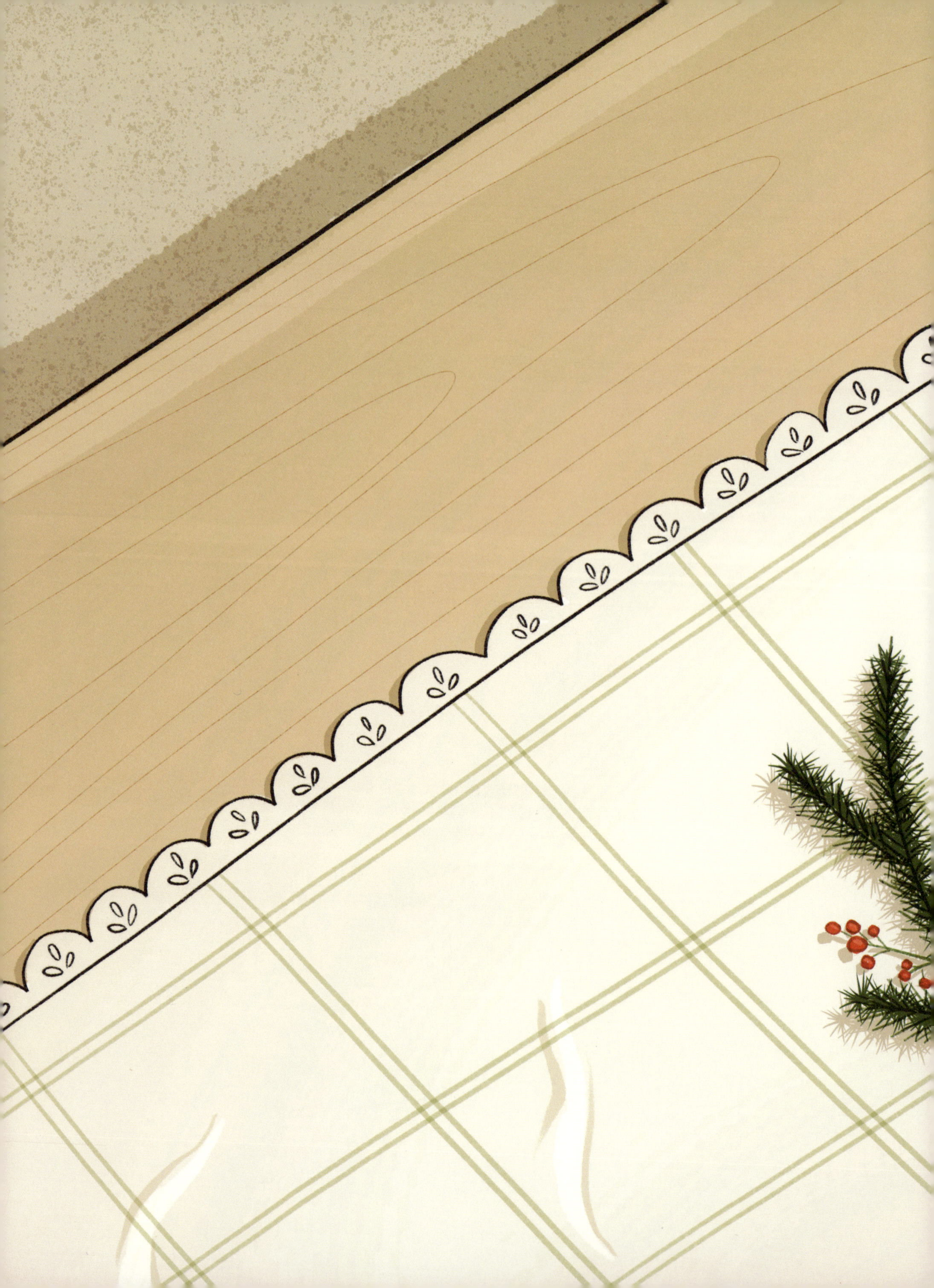

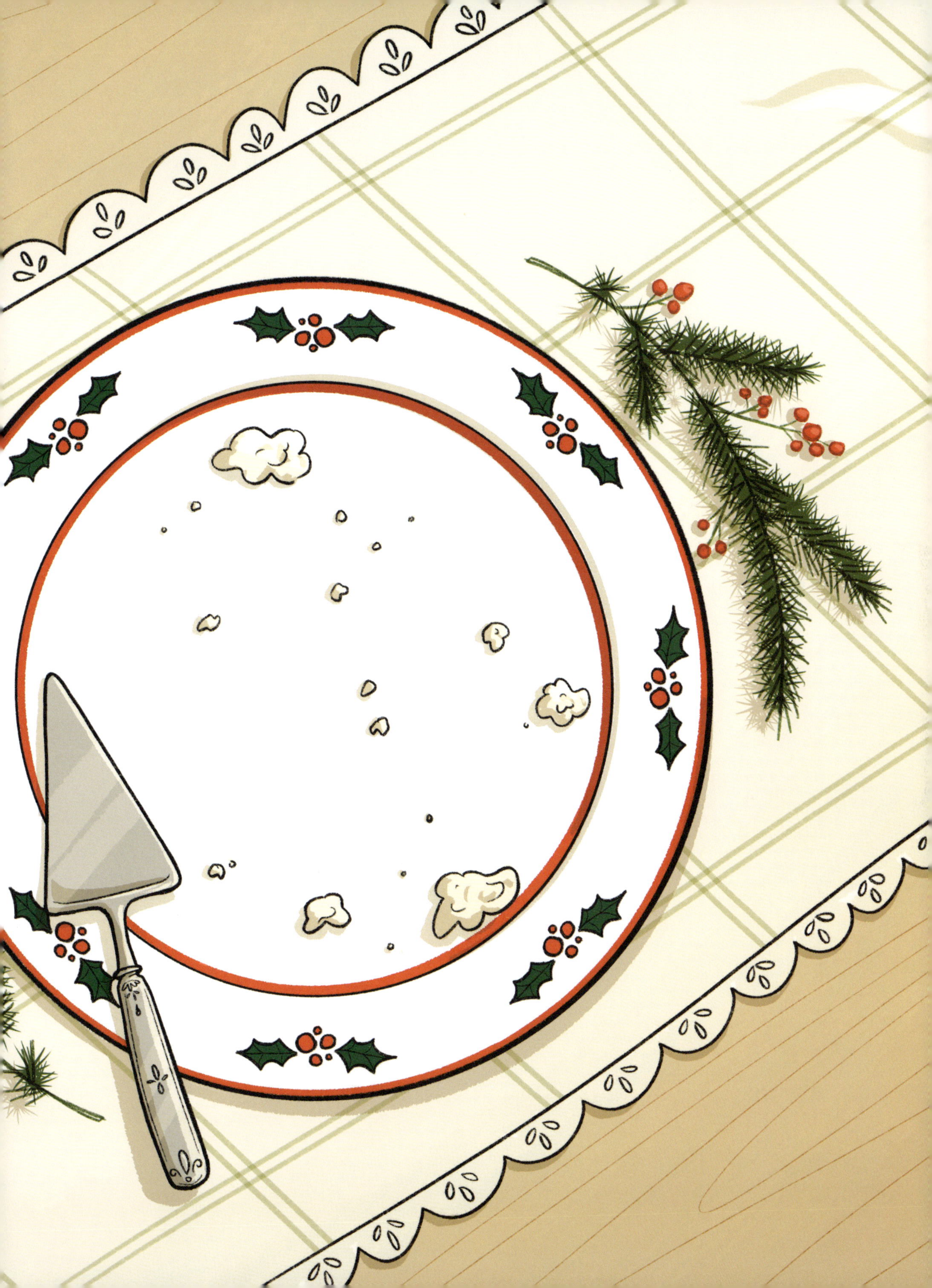

About the autor

Rose Bakewell is happily married to her husband, and together, they have three beautiful children and an adorable dog named Ollie.

Rose loves British history and is an award-winning author. She is an avid baker who was chosen to be a contestant on The Great American Baking Show in England and is the founder of **MRS. BAKEWELL'S**.
THE CREAM TEA COMPANY

Her inspiration for the Lottie book series is derived from her love of baking and wanting to create a comfy cozy feeling for those who read her books.